4TH GRADE GEOGRAPHY NORTH AND SOUTH POLES

The two poles are at extreme
opposites of the planet,
and many of their features
are also polar opposites.

NORTH POLE

The North Pole is the northernmost part of Earth. The North Pole is covered in a thick layer of ice around 6 to 9 feet thick.

If you stand at
the North Pole,
whichever
direction you
go in you are
heading south.

In the winter, temperatures average around -34 degrees Celsius. In the summer it is quite a bit warmer at 0 degrees Celsius.

SOUTH POLE

The South Pole
is situated on
the continent
of Antarctica.
During the South
Pole Winter it is
dark all the time.

The South Pole has a desert climate, almost never receiving any precipitation. Air humidity is near zero.

The South
Pole is close
to the coldest
place on Earth.
The coldest
temperature
recorded at
the South Pole
is -82.8 degrees
Celsius.